Seven Wonders of the
ANCIENT WORLD

Michael Woods and Mary B. Woods

Twenty-First Century Books

Minneapolis

To Barbara and James Ellenberger, Michael and Sheila Dominguez, and Virginia and Robert Mahlke

Twenty-First Century Books
A division of Lerner Publishing Group, Inc.
241 First Avenue North
Minneapolis, MN 55401 U.S.A.

Website address: www.lernerbooks.com

Library of Congress Cataloging-in-Publication Data

Woods, Michael, 1946–
    Seven wonders of the ancient world / by Michael Woods and Mary B. Woods.
        p.   cm. — (Seven wonders)
    Includes bibliographical references and index.
    ISBN 978–0–8225–7568–9 (lib. bdg. : alk. paper)
    1. Seven Wonders of the World—Juvenile literature. I. Woods, Mary B. (Mary Boyle), 1946– II. Title.
    N5333.W89 2009
    722—dc22   2007040828

Manufactured in the United States of America
1 2 3 4 5 6 – DP – 14 13 12 11 10 09

Contents

INTRODUCTION

*P*EOPLE LOVE TO MAKE LISTS OF THE BIGGEST AND THE BEST. ALMOST 2,500 YEARS AGO, A GREEK WRITER NAMED HERODOTUS (CA. 484–425 B.C.) MADE A LIST OF THE MOST AWESOME THINGS EVER BUILT BY PEOPLE. THE LIST INCLUDED BUILDINGS, STATUES, AND OTHER OBJECTS THAT WERE LARGE, WONDROUS, IMPRESSIVE, OR UNBELIEVABLE. OTHER WRITERS ADDED THEIR OWN IDEAS TO THE LIST. WRITERS EVENTUALLY AGREED ON A FINAL LIST. IT BECAME KNOWN AS THE SEVEN WONDERS OF THE ANCIENT WORLD. THE ANCIENT WONDERS WERE:

THE GREAT PYRAMID AT GIZA: *a tomb for an ancient Egyptian king. The pyramid still stands in Giza, Egypt.*

THE COLOSSUS OF RHODES: *a giant statue of Helios, the Greek sun god. The statue stood in Rhodes, an island in the Aegean Sea.*

THE LIGHTHOUSE AT ALEXANDRIA: *an enormous beacon to sailors at sea. It stood in the harbor at Alexandria, Egypt.*

THE HANGING GARDENS OF BABYLON: *magnificent gardens near the ancient city of Babylon (near modern-day Baghdad, Iraq).*

THE MAUSOLEUM AT HALICARNASSUS: *a marble tomb for a ruler in the Persian Empire. It was located in the ancient city of Halicarnassus (in modern Turkey).*

THE STATUE OF ZEUS AT OLYMPIA: *a statue honoring the king of the Greek gods. It stood in Olympia, Greece.*

THE TEMPLE OF ARTEMIS AT EPHESUS: *a temple honoring a Greek goddess. It stood on the coast of the Aegean Sea, in modern-day Turkey.*

Most of these ancient wonders are no longer standing. Wars, earthquakes, weather, and the passage of time destroyed them. But they stayed in people's imaginations a very long time. Through the ages, people continued to tell stories about the seven wonders and to imagine what they must have looked like.

A WONDERFUL PLACE

Herodotus and other writers of the original list did not go far to search for wonders. They did not visit ancient China, ancient Mexico, or ancient southern Africa to see the wonders of those lands. Most people in those days did not travel very far from home at all. So Herodotus's list includes wonders built by people who lived around or near his homeland in the eastern end of the Mediterranean Sea. The Mediterranean is surrounded by southern Europe (including Greece), northern Africa, and southwestern Asia.

Greece, Turkey, Iraq, Egypt, and other countries are home to some of the world's great civilizations. Civilizations are organized societies. They have governments, cities, roads, writing systems, art and culture, science, a steady food supply, and armies to protect themselves.

Mediterranean civilizations have given many gifts to the world. The ancient Greeks, for example, created a new system of government called a democracy. In democracies, citizens vote for their leaders. The Greek democratic system set an example for many modern governments around the world. These Mediterranean civilizations have also left their unique mark in art, music, theater, religion, architecture, philosophy, and many other fields.

A TRIP BACK IN TIME

Get ready to visit some of the wonders of the ancient world. *Ancient* is another word for "old"—so we will explore cities, temples, monuments, and other wonders from long ago. At one stop, we will see a building that was the tallest structure in the world for almost four thousand years. We will also stop to see giant statues of the Greek gods Zeus and Helios. Other stops will include a temple, a lighthouse, and an amazing garden in the middle of a desert. Get ready for adventure—and some surprises—as you set off on your tour of the ancient world.

1 THE Great Pyramid AT GIZA

Building on the Great Pyramid at Giza in Egypt began about 2550 B.C.

*F*OR THOUSANDS OF YEARS, ANCIENT EGYPT WAS RULED BY KINGS CALLED PHARAOHS. FOR MUCH OF THAT TIME, EGYPT WAS A RICH AND POWERFUL NATION. IT HELD INFLUENCE THROUGHOUT THE MIDDLE EAST AND CENTRAL AFRICA. AS RULERS OF THIS WEALTHY LAND, THE PHARAOHS LIVED VERY WELL. THEY HAD BEAUTIFUL PALACES AND TREASURES OF GOLD AND JEWELS. THEY ALSO BUILT ENORMOUS ROYAL TOMBS. THE MOST IMPRESSIVE OF THESE IS THE GREAT PYRAMID AT GIZA.

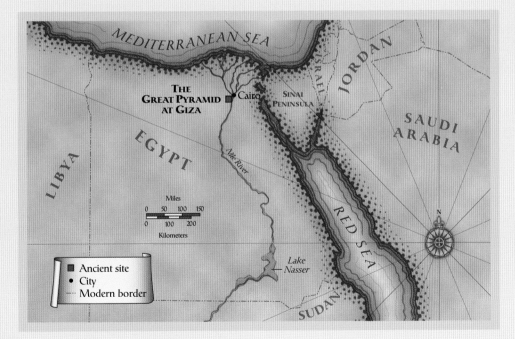

The afterlife was very important to the ancient Egyptians. This wall painting from an Egyptian tomb shows a funeral procession on the Nile River.

As soon as a pharaoh became king, he ordered workers to build his tomb. No matter how young a pharaoh was, he had to begin planning where his body would be buried after death.

The pharaoh did not expect to die soon. But Egyptian tombs often took a long time to build. Many workers and materials were needed, and each pharaoh wanted his tomb to be perfect. Some tombs were large complexes dug beneath Egypt's desert sands. Others were pyramids—enormous monuments several stories tall. The Great Pyramid at Giza is the largest pyramid ever built in Egypt.

TITANIC TOMBS

The history of Egypt's pharaohs is divided into dynasties. A dynasty is a family of rulers. Ancient Egypt had thirty-two dynasties of pharaohs. They ruled the land from about 2920 to 332 B.C.

Pharaohs in the earliest dynasties were buried in underground tombs. Workers

FAST *Fact*

The ancient Egyptians built more than fifty pyramids. But later, ancient Egyptians stopped building pyramids. One reason is that the large monuments were easy targets for robbers. The robbers would break into the pyramids and steal the pharaohs' treasures. In about the 1500s B.C., Egyptians began burying important people in underground tombs in the Valley of the Kings, a desert area in central Egypt.

KING *Sneferu*

Khufu's father, King Sneferu, built the first pyramid that had rooms aboveground. Before Sneferu built the Maidum Pyramid, pyramids were built over underground tombs. Built about 2600 B.C., Maidum had a burial chamber within its walls, not under it.

This ivory statue from the 2000s B.C. is of the Egyptian pharaoh Khufu.

covered the tops of the tombs with mounds of earth. Later, they began covering the tombs with rectangular buildings called mastabas. Mastabas had flat roofs and sloping walls. Builders experimented with the sloping structures, making them larger and taller. Over time, they created pyramids—four-sided structures that come to a point at the top.

Egyptologists (people who study ancient Egypt) do not think that builders used the pyramid shape by accident. They believe that the shape had special meaning. Some Egyptologists think that the pyramids were built to look like a sacred stone called the *benben*. In Egyptian myth, the benben was a hill—the first land to appear at the beginning of time. The sacred stone also represents the rays of the sun. Egyptians believed that pharaohs used sunrays to climb to heaven after death.

KHUFU'S GREAT PYRAMID

About 2551 B.C., the Egyptian pharaoh Khufu came to power. Khufu is also known by his Greek name, Cheops. He was the son of King Sneferu and Queen Hetepheres.

Soon after he became pharaoh, Khufu ordered his workers to begin building his pyramid. He chose to build at Giza, an area on the western side of the Nile River in northern Egypt. Giza was near the ancient Egyptian capital, Memphis. Present-day Giza is just outside the suburbs of Cairo, Egypt's modern capital.

Khufu was powerful enough to create a huge army of workers to build a special pyramid. For a long time, historians thought the Great Pyramid had been built by slaves. But modern Egyptologists think that Khufu's workers were paid volunteers. They believe that the workers were proud to take part in building the pharaoh's tomb.

The workers came from all over Egypt. Many were farmers. They worked on the pyramid during the seasons when they did not need to tend their crops. Khufu paid the workers and bought their food and water.

A BUSY *Place*

Architects and builders were not the only people at work at Giza. A whole village cropped up during the building of the Great Pyramid. Crews were set up to organize the workers. Officials were hired to make sure the workers were paid. Bakers, beer makers, and merchants set up shops to feed and clothe the workers. There was even a cemetery so that workers could be buried near the pyramid they had worked so hard to build.

A pharaoh (center on chair) *surveys the construction of his pyramid in this modern drawing.*

Building Blocks

The building of Khufu's pyramid began with his architects—people who design buildings. The architects first planned the base of the structure. The sides of the pyramid face exactly north, south, east, and west. After the architects had marked the base of the pyramid in the sand, workers began bringing in the building materials.

Each side of the Great Pyramid's base is almost 758 feet (231 meters) long. The base would cover ten modern football fields. The builders needed many, many stone building blocks to create a structure that large. Some of the limestone (a white or grayish rock) came from nearby quarries (places where stone is dug or cut from the ground). But some of the granite quarries were far to the south of Giza.

Most of the blocks used to build Khufu's pyramid weigh about 2.5 tons (2.3 metric tons) each. Some of them weigh 70 tons (64 metric tons). That is almost twice the weight of a modern eighteen-wheel truck. How did Khufu's workers get these enormous stones to the building site?

Egyptologists believe that the stone blocks from farther away were shipped down the Nile on boats. When the blocks arrived at Giza, workers loaded them onto sledges. Sledges are strong, heavy wooden sleds. Instead of wheels, they have runners (metal or wooden rails) along the bottom. The sledges also carried the stone from the nearby quarries.

Archaeologists (scientists who study the buildings, tools, and other artifacts of ancient civilizations) are not sure exactly how the sledges were used. Workers may have pulled the sledges over a road made from wooden boards. Another idea is that the sledges were rolled over poles laid down on the ground. These poles looked like modern telephone poles. A little oil on the boards or poles would have made the pulling easier.

Lifting the Blocks

After the first blocks arrived at the pyramid site, workers built the base. Then they added the second layer of stone blocks. As the building walls rose, workers had to lift the huge stones higher and higher.

Archaeologists have several ideas about how builders lifted the blocks. One main idea is that workers built dirt ramps along the sides of the pyramid.

> *"After laying the stones for the base, they raised the remaining stones to their places by means of machines formed of short wooden planks."*
>
> — *Herodotus, an ancient Greek historian who wrote about the pyramids ca. 450 B.C.*

Workers rolled blocks up the ramp and into position on the pyramid wall.

When they were ready to begin the next layer, workers added more dirt to the ramp to make it higher. After the pyramid was finished, workers removed the dirt ramp with shovels. Other archaeologists, however, say that it would have been too difficult to build and use these ramps.

A PERFECT FIT

After the pyramid walls were finished, workers covered them in white, polished limestone. At the tip of the pyramid, they placed a special block. That block was covered in gold or in a mix of gold and silver. Khufu's tomb was an amazing sight—standing 481 feet (147 m) high and gleaming white above the brown sands.

It took workers more than twenty years to finish the Great Pyramid. The pyramid's 2.3 million stone blocks weighed more than 6 million tons (5.4 metric tons). Khufu's workers did a very good job fitting those blocks together. They still fit so tightly that a modern visitor cannot slip a knife blade into the joints between most of the blocks.

But the pyramid was not the only building Khufu built at Giza. Nearby he built three small pyramids for his wives. He also built two temples—one for his funeral and one where people could worship him after his death. To the south, he built mastabas and other tombs for important people in his kingdom.

SHRINKING *Pyramid*

In ancient times, the Great Pyramid was larger than it is in modern times. The pyramid was 481 feet (147 m) high. Each side of the base was 758 feet (231 m) long. But during the A.D. 1300s and 1400s, the limestone covering was removed and taken away to help build the city of Cairo. Without the covering, the pyramid shrank to its current size—450 feet (137 m) high and 755 feet (230 m) long on each side.

After Khufu died, his son Khafre became pharaoh. Khafre had his own pyramid built just southwest of the Great Pyramid. Khafre's pyramid is not as large as his father's. But Khafre added his own monument to the site. In front of his pyramid sits the Great Sphinx—a huge stone lion with a human head. When Khafre's son Menkaura became pharaoh, he also built a pyramid near his father's tomb. The pyramids of all three pharaohs and their wives still stand at Giza.

Khufu's son Khafre and grandson Menkaura also built pyramids at Giza. The large pyramid on the left is Menkaura's. The large center pyramid is Khafre's. The three smaller pyramids in front were built by Menkaura for his wives.

FAST *Fact*

In some photographs of Giza, Khafre's pyramid looks larger than the Great Pyramid. That is an optical illusion—a trick of the eye. Khafre's pyramid looks bigger because it was built on higher ground than the Great Pyramid. In reality, it is 32 feet (9.8 m) shorter than the Great Pyramid.

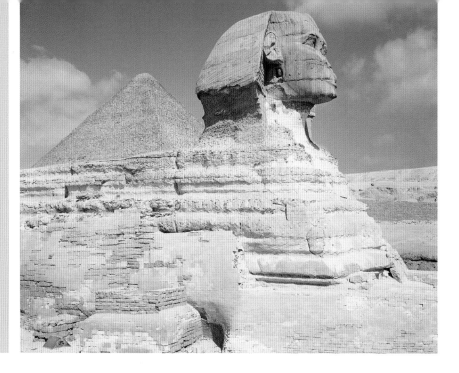

Khafre built the Great Sphinx during his reign (2500s B.C.). The pyramid in the background is the Great Pyramid.

A WORLD WONDER

The Great Pyramid was the tallest building in the world for almost 4,900 years. Even in ancient times, it drew tourists awed by its size and beauty. Herodotus visited Giza in about 450 B.C. He listened to local stories about how the pyramid had been built and how many workers it had taken to build. Herodotus was so impressed by the stories that he included Khufu and the pyramid in his book *The Histories*.

Modern Egyptologists think that some of what Herodotus wrote about Giza is incorrect. For example, he said that Khufu was a cruel ruler. But other Egyptian sources do not match that story. Modern scientists also

A LONG-STANDING *Record*

The Great Pyramid was the world's tallest building for thousands of years. No one built anything higher until A.D. 1310. That year workers finished the central tower on Lincoln Cathedral in England *(below)*. The tower and its spire were 525 feet (160 m) high.

think some of Herodotus's details of the pyramid's construction are wrong. Still, Herodotus's book made Giza famous in ancient Greece. When a list of the Seven Wonders of the World was created, ancient historians included the Great Pyramid.

Even in our age of skyscrapers, the Great Pyramid is still an amazing sight. Over the centuries, the Great Pyramid has lost most of its white limestone covering. But it towers over the desert floor along with the other ancient buildings at Giza. Thousands of tourists from all over the world visit the Great Pyramid each year. It is the only one of the original Seven Wonders of the World that still exists.

Tourism and time have taken a toll on the buildings at Giza. The body heat and breath of visitors touring the inside of the Great Pyramid has raised the humidity (the amount of water in the air). The high humidity was beginning to damage the walls. Egyptian authorities did not want to keep visitors away. But they had to begin limiting the number allowed inside the pyramid. They also installed machines to control humidity.

No Climbing

Below: *This view from the base shows the height of the Great Pyramid.* Right: *A tourist ignores a sign and climbs the Great Pyramid. The pyramid is like a giant staircase, but climbers damage the monument.*

WONDERING ABOUT KHUFU

Egyptologists continue to study the Great Pyramid. They have mapped out and explored the burial chambers inside the pyramid. They have also mapped the whole complex at Giza and uncovered some buried buildings.

But one thing they have not found is the body of Khufu. Because of their religious beliefs, ancient Egyptians preserved dead bodies to keep them from rotting after death. Ancient Egyptians believed that a person, especially a pharaoh, needed his body for life in the afterworld. So most pharaohs were made into mummies—preserved bodies wrapped in linens and placed in decorated coffins. In the afterworld, the pharaoh also needed his jewels, money, food, and other items. All the pharaoh's treasures were placed in the tomb with the mummy.

Archaeologists have found other Egyptian mummies—the mummy of King Tutankhamen, for example. And they found Khufu's red granite coffin. But no trace of Khufu's mummy has ever been found. The mystery only adds to the wonder of the Great Pyramid at Giza.

EVER *Wonder?*

Why didn't the 6-million-ton (5.4-million-metric-ton) Great Pyramid sink into the desert sands? The answer is that just under the sand is a thick layer of hard rock. Giza sits on a plateau (a flat area raised above the land around it) of limestone.

Visitors to the Great Pyramid gaze down at the ruins that surround it. (Visitors are no longer allowed to climb the Great Pyramid because they might damage it.) Khafre's pyramid is in the background.

2 The Colossus
OF RHODES

This German engraving of the Colossus of Rhodes (a Greek island) is from the late nineteenth century.

COLOSSUS IS FROM A GREEK WORD
MEANING "STATUE." THE COLOSSUS OF RHODES WAS A HUGE FIGURE
OF THE ANCIENT GREEK GOD HELIOS. HELIOS IS THE GOD OF THE
SUN. HIS COLOSSUS STOOD ON THE ISLAND OF RHODES, PART OF
THE MODERN COUNTRY OF GREECE.

    The Colossus of Rhodes stood at or near the entrance to Mandraki
Harbor. The harbor is on the east side of the city of Rhodes, at the
northeastern tip of the island.

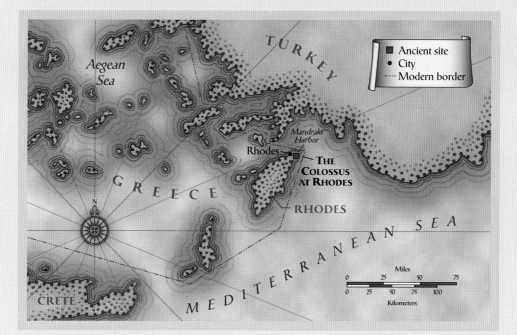

A THANK-YOU NOTE

Why did the ancient Greeks place a statue of Helios in the harbor? The statue was a thank-you note from the people of Rhodes. They were thanking Helios for helping them win a war.

The war began after Alexander the Great (356–323 B.C.) died. Alexander was a Greek ruler born in the Macedonian region of Greece. He conquered many lands outside Greece. Rhodes was one land that Alexander took over. After Alexander's death, his generals fought for control of Alexander's conquered lands. One of the generals was Ptolemy I Soter (367–282 B.C.). Another was Antigonus I (382–301 B.C.). The people of Rhodes supported Ptolemy.

AN ANGRY GENERAL

In 306 B.C., Ptolemy declared himself king of Egypt. Antigonus, meanwhile, fought for control of other lands in the eastern part of the Mediterranean. He set his sights on Rhodes. Rhodes controlled the entrance to the Aegean Sea and was an import center for shipping and trade. Antigonus ordered his son, Demetrius (337–283 B.C.), to attack Rhodes.

In 305 B.C., Demetrius began his attack on Rhodes. He had an army of forty thousand soldiers. Rhodes only had about seven thousand fighting men. But the city of Rhodes was surrounded by a high, thick wall. Demetrius's army had to get over that wall to conquer the people of Rhodes.

Demetrius decided to build a wooden tower so tall he could use it to attack the city. Such towers are called siege towers. A siege is a battle waged against a protected place, such as a castle or a walled city.

Demetrius's army built the siege tower on six large boats tied together. The tower was large enough to hold many soldiers and battle equipment. They sailed the tower toward the city of Rhodes, ready to attack. But a sudden sea storm knocked over the tower, and the army turned back.

This coin from the third century B.C. bears the image of Egyptian king and general Ptolemy I Soter.

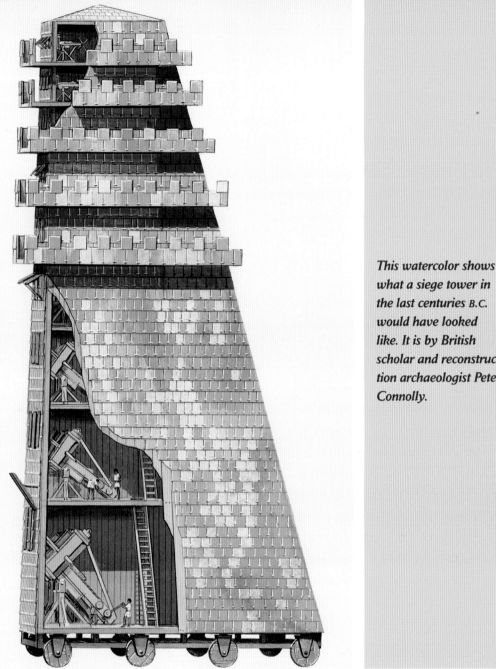

This watercolor shows what a siege tower in the last centuries B.C. would have looked like. It is by British scholar and reconstruction archaeologist Peter Connolly.

The army built a second wooden siege tower more than 100 feet (30 m) high. This time they mounted it on iron wheels. They rolled the siege tower against Rhodes's wall. Soldiers climbed to the top of the tower and shot arrows over the wall.

The soldiers on the tower also had catapults. These war machines were like giant slingshots. They hurled heavy rocks and burning chunks of wood into the city of Rhodes. The people of Rhodes fought back and prayed to Helios to help them.

The siege went on like this for almost one year. Finally, Ptolemy sent soldiers to help the people of Rhodes. Antigonus gave up the battle and told Demetrius to declare peace. Demetrius and his army went home in 304 B.C.

BUILDING A COLOSSUS

The people of Rhodes believed that Helios had helped them fight off Demetrius's army. They wanted to thank Helios. They chose a sculptor, Chares, to create a great statute in honor of the god.

In 294 B.C., Chares and his builders began. They first created a marble platform for the statue. They then built several stone columns that would form the middle of the statue. All over the stone columns, they inserted iron rods.

Chares next had to create the statue's outer skin. He cast metal plates that he would form into the statue's feet, hands, head, and other body parts. To cast metal, workers heat it until it is liquid. Then they pour it into a mold. As the metal cools, it hardens into the shape of the mold. The workers then remove the mold from the metal piece.

Chares already had much of the material needed for the statue. Demetrius left behind swords and other metal weapons. Workers in

THE NEW Colossus

In 1886 French artist Frederic Auguste Bartholdi and his workers built the Statue of Liberty (below) on an island in the harbor of New York City. The 305-foot (93 m)-tall statue faces the Atlantic Ocean with a glowing torch lifted up to the sky. When ships were the most common way to travel, the statue served as a beacon, or guiding light. It welcomed immigrants and other travelers into the harbor.

In 1883 an American poet named Emma Lazarus wrote about the Statue of Liberty. In her poem "The New Colossus," Lazarus compared the monument to the Colossus of Rhodes. Lazarus wrote that the Colossus of Rhodes belonged to the ancient world, while the Statue of Liberty belonged to the New World.

COLOSSAL Word

The word *colossus* originally just meant "statue." It was used for any statue, even doll-sized statues. The meaning changed after the people of Rhodes built their statue. From then on, people used the word *colossus* to mean anything gigantic.

This painting of the colossus closely represents how historians think the statue actually looked. The painting was created by Salvador Dali in 1954.

Rhodes melted down the metal. They also bought more bronze, copper, and iron from places throughout the Mediterranean world.

Demetrius also left behind the siege tower. Workers stood on the tower as they put the statue together. They began by attaching the metal body parts to the iron rods. It took twelve years to finish. But by 282 B.C., the colossus stood guard over Rhodes.

A HARBOR GUARDIAN

No one is sure exactly where the colossus stood. Some pictures show the statue at the entrance to the harbor. In these pictures, Helios is straddling the harbor's entrance. One foot is on each side of the harbor entrance. Ships are sailing through the colossus's legs.

But historians think those pictures are wrong. Helios could not have straddled the entrance. It would not have been possible to make a statue that tall, with legs long enough for ships to sail under. Archaeologists think the colossus probably stood to one side of the entrance. Its legs were probably together to make the statue more stable.

A COLOSSAL EARTHQUAKE

The colossus stood for only about fifty-six years. In about 225 B.C., a terrible earthquake struck Rhodes. The quake destroyed most of the buildings in Rhodes. As the ground below the colossus shook, the statue's knees snapped. The giant form fell to the ground in pieces.

COLOSSUS VS. Liberty

Both the Colossus of Rhodes and the Statue of Liberty had bodies about the same height. Liberty, however, is taller because of her raised arm. Liberty also stands on a higher pedestal (base).

We might have never known any details of the Colossus of Rhodes if not for the Roman writer Pliny the Elder (A.D. 23–79). Pliny visited Rhodes and saw the colossus lying in ruins. He described the statue and measured parts of it. Historians also know how the ancient Greeks depicted Helios from other statues and artwork.

The colossus's body was probably about 110 feet (34 m) high. It stood on a platform 50 feet (15 m) high. The statue wore a spiked crown—a symbol of the rays of the sun. One hand shaded its eyes, and the other hand held a cloak.

The Colossus of Rhodes wore no clothes. The statue's metal skin was polished and gleamed in the sun. People must have been able to see it from a great distance.

A WONDER

The Colossus of Rhodes lay where it fell for almost nine hundred years. People came to Rhodes from all around the region to see the fallen wonder. They could walk right into the hollow body where it had broken apart at the knees.

" Few people can make their arms meet round the thumb of the statue and the fingers are bigger than most [other] statues. "

—Pliny the Elder, a Roman writer who saw the colossus in ruins in the first century A.D.

MODERN *Rhodes*

Almost 120,000 people live on the island of Rhodes. Many of them live in the island's biggest city, also called Rhodes. Thousands of tourists come to Rhodes each year. Visitors can walk to the entrance of Rhodes's famous harbor. Statues of two deer stand on each side of the harbor entrance. They mark the spots where the colossus's feet might have stood.

In A.D. 654, Arab armies conquered Rhodes. They broke up the larger pieces of the colossus. The pieces were carted away on camels and sold as scrap metal. But the great statue of Helios lived on in the imagination of the Mediterranean peoples. It was a beautiful work of art and an amazing feat of engineering. When the list of Seven Wonders was drawn up, the colossus found a place among the other incredible monuments of the ancient world.

On Rhodes, the Fortress of Saint Nicholas stands in the harbor where the colossus once stood.

3 The Lighthouse AT ALEXANDRIA

This German engraving of the Lighthouse at Alexandria in Egypt is from the late nineteenth century.

ONLY ONE WONDER OF THE ANCIENT WORLD HAD A PRACTICAL USE. MOST WONDERS WERE BUILT TO HONOR A GOD OR AN IMPORTANT PERSON. THE FAMOUS LIGHTHOUSE AT ALEXANDRIA IN EGYPT WAS BUILT TO HELP PEOPLE.

Lighthouses are tall buildings with bright lights on top. They light up safe routes into harbors. Lighthouses also mark dangerous spots along the shore. Some of those dangers include rocks or shallow water that can sink ships. The Lighthouse at Alexandria was the first lighthouse in recorded history.

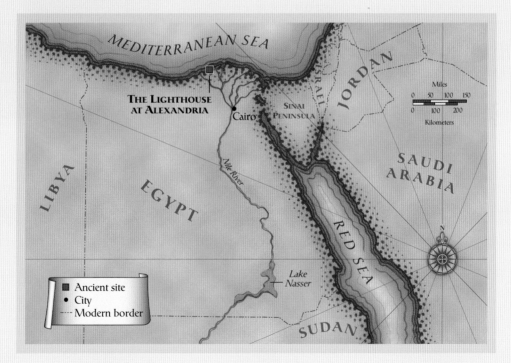

MADE TO USE

In 332 B.C., Alexander the Great founded
the city of Alexandria. He chose to
build the city in northern Egypt, close to
where the Nile River empties into the
Mediterranean Sea. But Alexander died
before he could finish Alexandria. When
Ptolemy I Soter became the new ruler of
Egypt, he finished building the city.

Alexandria became one of the busiest
seaports in the ancient world. Many ships
sailed into its two harbors. One harbor was
on the Nile River. The second harbor was
on the Mediterranean. Merchants around
the Mediterranean shipped goods through
those harbors. Ptolemy realized the city
needed something to help direct all that sea
traffic safely into the harbors.

But Alexandria's shore was very flat.
No tall hills or rocky cliffs marked the land
for sailors at sea. About 290 B.C., Ptolemy
decided that he would build a landmark. It
would help ships find the harbor.

Ptolemy knew his landmark would have to be very tall. Sailors would
be able to see it before they ever hit the rocks close to shore. He decided to
build a tower on the small island of Pharos just outside the city. Ptolemy hired
Sostratus of Cnidos, a Greek architect born in modern-day Turkey. Sostratus
began working on plans for the tower at once.

*This modern bronze statue of Alexander the
Great stands in Thessaloniki, Macedonia,
Greece. Alexander, a Greek ruler, conquered
Egypt in the 300s B.C.*

"*[Alexander] chanced one night in his sleep to see a
wonderful vision; a gray-headed old man . . . seemed
to stand by him and pronounce these verses: 'An
island lies where loud billows roar, Pharos they call
it, on the Egyptian shore.'*"

—*Plutarch (ca. A.D. 46–120),* The Life of Alexander the Great, *describing
Alexander's dream of where to build the city of Alexandria, Egypt*

FIRE IN THE SKY

Ptolemy did not just want his tower to be practical. He wanted it to be a symbol of the great city of Alexandria. He wanted the tower to be gigantic and beautiful. It would be something people would recognize and admire.

Sostratus worked hard to meet Ptolemy's demands. He designed a tower almost 400 feet (122 m) high—as high as a forty-story skyscraper. It was built in three parts. The lower part was shaped like a modern office building. It was square and sturdy. The second part was smaller and sat centered on the first. According to some stories, this part of the tower was octagonal (eight-sided).

This modern illustration of the Lighthouse at Alexandria shows the legendary octagonal second story.

The first and second parts had ramps and staircases by which people could reach the third and highest part of the tower. Inside this third part was a huge mirror. Historians think the mirror may have been made of polished metal. During the day, the mirror caught the strong Mediterranean sunlight. At night, workers built a huge fire in front of the mirror. The mirror reflected and magnified the glow of the fire.

Humans had been building signal fires for a very long time. People had built fires on tops of mountains or towers to warn that enemies were approaching. People had even built bonfires on hills surrounding a harbor to warn and guide ships. But this was the first time in history that a tower, a mirror, and a fire had been used in this way.

Some historians think Sostratus topped off his tower with an enormous statue. It may have been a statue of Poseidon, the Greek god of the sea. Or it may have been Poseidon's brother Zeus, the king of the Greek gods.

SMELLY *Fires*

The lighthouse fire at Alexandria probably did not smell very good. Firewood was hard to find and was expensive in Egypt, and the lighthouse fire needed a lot of fuel. So it was not unusual for lighthouse keepers to burn manure (dried animal waste).

ANCIENT TOURIST ATTRACTION

It took Sostratus twenty years to finish the lighthouse. In that time, Ptolemy I died. His son Ptolemy II took over as ruler of Egypt. He dedicated and officially opened the finished lighthouse in 285 B.C. Egypt then contained the two tallest buildings on Earth—the Great Pyramid at Giza and the Lighthouse at Alexandria.

People from around the region came to see the amazing lighthouse. The second part of its tower included observation decks. People could stand on these balconies and get a fantastic view of the sea. In those days, the lighthouse was the only building in the world with such a view. The tourists may have even been able to buy miniature versions of the lighthouse as souvenirs.

"Sostratus of Cnidos, son of Dexiphanes, to the savior gods, for sailors."

—Sostratus's dedication carved in the wall of the Lighthouse at Alexandria, 285 B.C.

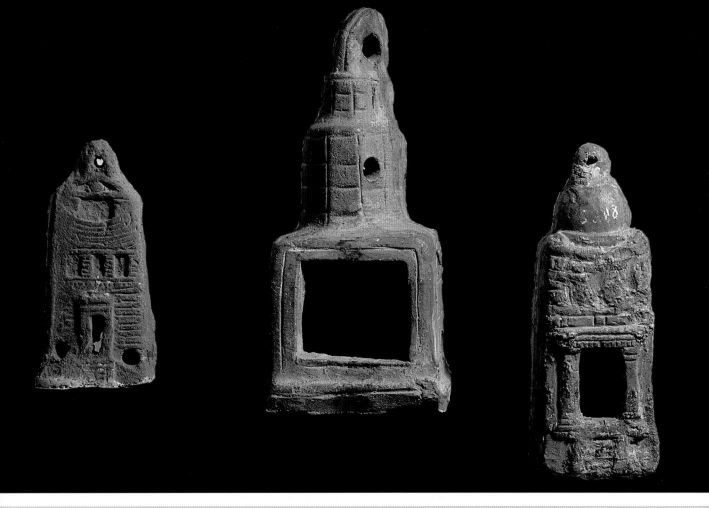

Above: *These ancient ceramic lamps were made to look like the Lighthouse at Alexandria.* Below: *This Roman coin shows a ship approaching the Lighthouse at Alexandria. This coin was minted in Alexandria in the second century* A.D.

EVER *Wonder?*

How do modern historians know what the Lighthouse at Alexandria looked like? They do not know exactly. But they have a pretty good idea because of the lighthouse's popularity. Images of the famous monument appeared in ancient artwork and on ancient Greek and Roman coins. Archaeologists have even found small stone lanterns meant to look like the lighthouse.

But the lighthouse was not only amazing as a tourist attraction. For more than one thousand years, it guided sailors safely into Alexandria's busy harbor. The light from the lighthouse could be seen 35 miles (56 kilometers) out to sea. The technology was amazing for its time.

LIGHTS OUT

It is also amazing that the lighthouse stood for so long. It withstood the salt air, sea storms, and the Mediterranean sun. But nature did eventually take its toll. In about A.D. 795, an earthquake knocked over the top part of the lighthouse. More earthquakes damaged the walls of the remaining stories. Finally, a severe earthquake—possibly in about A.D. 1303—knocked the lighthouse over.

Some of the lighthouse's huge building stones crashed into the waters around Pharos. Others fell to the ground and were recycled for another building project. In 1480 the ruler of Egypt, Sultan Quait Bey, decided to build a military fort to protect Alexandria. He built Fort Quaitbey over the site of the

This fortress, known as Fort Quaitbey, stands on the edge of the modern city of Alexandria, Egypt, on the spot where the lighthouse once stood.

lighthouse. Workers used the lighthouse stones to help build the fort.

But as one of the Seven Wonders of the Ancient World, the Lighthouse at Alexandria was not forgotten. Greek historians, Egyptian writers, and Arab travelers all told tales of the amazing lighthouse.

REDISCOVERING A WONDER

Underwater archaeologists rediscovered the lighthouse in 1994. These scientists use scuba diving equipment to study ancient artifacts that are underwater. Special sensors and other instruments help them locate artifacts buried below the ocean bottom.

French and Egyptian archaeologists used those instruments to search the seafloor around Fort Quaitbey. The scientists found huge stone blocks. The blocks were in layers, as if deposited as the walls of a building toppled into the sea.

Scientists think those blocks were from the Lighthouse at Alexandria. Some of the blocks were a wonder in themselves. They were the biggest ever used in ancient construction. These blocks were 20 feet (6.1 m) long and 8 feet (2.4 m) wide. Each one weighed 20 tons (18 metric tons).

4

THE
Hanging Gardens
OF BABYLON

This American illustration from the 1930s, showing the Hanging Gardens of Babylon (in modern-day Iraq), was created for a book on wonders of the ancient world.

$\mathcal{W}$HEN A TRAVELER RETURNED FROM THE CITY OF BABYLON, OTHER PEOPLE CROWDED AROUND. THEY WANTED TO HEAR ABOUT THAT CITY. PEOPLE HEARING THE STORIES ALMOST ACHED TO VISIT BABYLON THEMSELVES.

Babylon was the capital city of Babylonia, part of an ancient Middle East region called Mesopotamia. In ancient times, Babylon was known as the most amazing, exciting city on Earth. Babylon was most famous for its fantastic gardens. Those gardens were one of the Seven Wonders of the Ancient World.

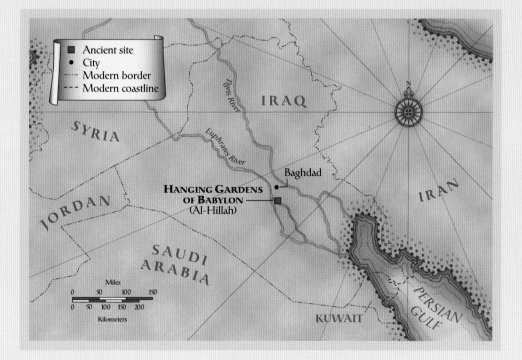

FIT FOR A KING

How could gardens be so famous? Part of the reason is the gardens' location in Mesopotamia. The region included lands that became modern Iraq and parts of Syria and Turkey. Babylon was about 55 miles (90 km) south of Baghdad, Iraq's capital city.

Some parts of Mesopotamia are very fertile, or good for farming. Those farms produced a steady supply of food. That drew more people to the region, and in time, the land became home to some of the world's major ancient civilizations.

But Babylon was in the middle of a very dry desert region. In the desert parts of Mesopotamia, rainwater was scarce. To grow plants in the dry soil, farmers had to irrigate, or bring water in by artificial means. Mesopotamian farmers brought water from the nearby Euphrates River or from underground wells.

The dry climate of what was once known as Mesopotamia makes it difficult for vegetation to grow without a water source such as the Euphrates River (below) or irrigation.

Hauling that water was difficult. So farmers saved their land to grow food that they could eat themselves or sell. But kings had servants to haul water and were rich enough that they did not need to sell farm crops. So kings began using their land to grow things just for enjoyment. They created royal gardens with beautiful, sweet-smelling flowers. The gardens also had blossoming vines and fruit trees. But even kings had only small gardens because water was so precious.

WONDER BUILDER

King Nebuchadnezzar II, however, built huge gardens in Babylon. Nebuchadnezzar became king of Babylon in 605 B.C. He ruled for forty-three years.

This king was a powerful general. Nebuchadnezzar fought many wars and destroyed his enemies. The Bible mentions that Nebuchadnezzar destroyed the Temple in Jerusalem. He forced the Jewish people to leave Jerusalem. Nebuchadnezzar brought them to Babylon.

At home this king built Babylon into a wonder. Ancient writers tell us that Nebuchadnezzar built the huge gardens, known as the Hanging Gardens, to cheer up his wife, Amyitis.

Amyitis belonged to a people called the Medes. The Medes lived in the northern part of present-day Iran. The land of the Medes was rugged country with mountains, hills, and green plants. It was much different from the flat, brown land in Babylon.

When Amyitis moved to Babylon, she became sad and homesick. Nebuchadnezzar wanted to cheer her up by creating scenery that would remind her of her home. About 600 B.C., he ordered workers to build the Hanging Gardens.

"Babylon surpasses in splendor any city in the known world."

—*Greek historian Herodotus, ca. 450 B.C.*

WONDER WALLS

The Hanging Gardens were enclosed within the city walls of Babylon. In those days, cities built walls as protection against invading armies. Workers did not have cranes or other machines for building. So city walls often were fairly low. Babylon's walls, however, may have been as high as 320 feet (98 m). That is higher than a thirty-story building. The walls may have been 80 feet (26 m) thick and 56 miles (90 km) long.

Other city walls in Mesopotamia were made from mud bricks. But parts of Babylon's walls had brightly colored bricks. Some bricks had the faces of lions, bulls, and dragons. Inside the walls, Babylon was filled with fantastic palaces, temples, and other buildings.

EVER Wonder?

Who were the Babylonians? They were Semitic people who lived in ancient Mesopotamia. *Semitic* means that they belonged to a large group of people who settled in ancient southwest Asia, or the modern-day Middle East. The Babylonians lived in Mesopotamia from about 1700 to 600 B.C. Most Babylonians were farmers, but they organized themselves around several cities. Babylon was the capital city and center of Babylonia.

This seventeenth-century painting shows ancient Babylon.

This wall, a part of Nebuchadnezzar's southern palace, was built in the sixth century B.C.

WRONG WORD WONDER

Why was Amyitis's retreat known as the Hanging Gardens? Historians do not think the gardens were really hanging from anything. They were not attached to ropes as hanging flower baskets are.

The mistaken idea began when someone translated a word from Greek into English. Greek writers described the gardens with a word that means "hanging." However, that word also means "overhanging."

The vines and other plants probably hung over terraces (steplike platforms). They were like plants hanging over the railing of a modern balcony or sundeck. But these hanging gardens were much bigger than a sundeck. The terraces formed a huge structure. The ancient Greek historian Diodorus described the gardens around 50 B.C. He said they were 400 feet (122 m) wide, 400 feet (122 m) long, and 80 feet (24 m) high.

BUILDING A WONDER

We know little about how the gardens were built. Three Greek writers did describe the gardens. Here is what the writer Strabo said in about A.D. 10:

> It consists of vaulted [covered by an arch or dome] terraces raised one above the other, and resting upon cube-shaped pillars. These are hollow and filled with earth to allow trees of the largest size to be planted. The pillars, the vaults, and terraces are constructed of baked brick and asphalt.

Workers probably first built frames for the terraces. The frames may have looked like huge boxes. Soil was piled into the spots where trees and plants would grow.

Gardeners then began planting. Nebuchadnezzar was very rich. He could afford to buy the most beautiful plants from around the world. Vines with brilliantly colored flowers hung over the sides of the terraces. On top of the terraces, trees and other plants grew. There may have been sweet-smelling cedar and cypress trees.

Amyitis and other members of the royal family could walk through the gardens. When they got hungry, they could pick pears, plums, and grapes

THE TOWER of Babel

Babylon was home to another famous ancient monument—the Tower of Babel *(shown below in a fifteenth-century French illustration)*. Babel was an early name for Babylon. Archaeologists think the Tower of Babel was a ziggurat to the Babylonian god Marduk. A ziggurat is a type of pyramid. Each layer is smaller than the one before, so the pyramid looks as if it is made of giant steps. Babylon's ziggurat to Marduk was the highest and most famous one in the world. It is even mentioned in the Old Testament.

This modern engraving reconstructs how scholars think a cross section of the hanging gardens would have looked.

from the garden's trees and vines. They probably relaxed in the shade of the trees. The gardens provided a cool and pleasant break from the desert heat and sand.

KEEPING THE GARDENS ALIVE

One of the biggest mysteries about the Hanging Gardens is how they stayed green. The plants were in a very dry desert. How did gardeners water the plants? Archaeologists know that ancient people in Mesopotamia had machines to irrigate the desert. One machine was the chain pump.

A chain pump is made from a chain or rope running over two wheels. Buckets are attached to the chain. One wheel sits in a body of water such as a river. As workers turn that wheel, the buckets scoop up water from the river. They carry it to the plants. As the buckets go around the other wheel, they tip and dump the water onto the ground.

For the Hanging Gardens, buckets may have emptied into a pool or irrigation ditch on the top terraces. Water flowed from there to the rest of the garden.

WONDERING ABOUT A WONDER

Modern archaeologists wonder about how the gardens were built. They imagine how this wonder really looked. Some of these scientists even question whether the gardens really existed.

They say stories about the gardens may have been made up by ancient writers. But some evidence seems to show that the gardens really existed. That evidence comes from the work of German archaeologist Robert Koldewey (1855–1925).

In the early 1900s, Koldewey excavated (dug up) many parts of the ancient city of Babylon. He found the ruins of the city walls, palaces, and an ancient roadway. Then he discovered the ruins of the foundation of another ancient building. The foundation was built with the same type of stone historians said builders had used at the Hanging Gardens of Babylon. Koldewey was sure he had found the basement storage rooms of Amyitis's gardens.

But not all modern archaeologists agree with Koldewey. Some still believe that evidence of the real gardens has never been found. For that reason, the Hanging Gardens of Babylon remains one of the most mysterious of the Seven Wonders of the Ancient World.

THE CODE OF Hammurabi

One early king of Babylonia, Hammurabi, became a very famous name in history. Hammurabi probably lived in the 1700s B.C. He created a set of laws called the Code of Hammurabi. It listed laws about many areas of community life—such as doing business, borrowing money, farming, and getting married. The laws were written down so that people knew how they were expected to behave. They also understood how they would be punished if they did not follow the laws. The code was based on older customs among Semitic tribes.

In 1902 French archaeologists found a stone copy of the Code of Hammurabi in Iran. Studying the code has helped historians understand ancient Middle Eastern civilizations. The stone copy is on display in the Louvre Museum in Paris, France.

Above: *Some archaeologists believe these foundations held Amyitis's gardens.* Below: *This seventeenth-century Austrian fresco (plaster-based wall painting) shows the Hanging Gardens of Babylon.*

MVRVS BABYLONI

5 The Mausoleum
AT HALICARNASSUS

This French painting is of the Mausoleum at Halicarnassus (in modern-day Turkey).

𝕸ODERN-DAY PEOPLE AROUND THE WORLD HAVE MANY DIFFERENT CUSTOMS FOR FUNERALS AND BURIALS OF THE DEAD. IN WESTERN COUNTRIES, MANY PEOPLE ARE BURIED IN CEMETERIES. MOST PEOPLE ARE BURIED IN COFFINS IN UNDERGROUND GRAVES. BUT SOME OLDER CEMETERIES ALSO HAVE BUILDINGS THAT SERVE AS TOMBS. THESE BUILDINGS ARE CALLED MAUSOLEUMS.

The word *mausoleum* comes from one of the Seven Wonders of the Ancient World. That wonder was the tomb of King Mausolus. In the 300s B.C., Mausolus ruled lands in what became the modern country of Turkey.

KING MAUSOLUS

Mausolus's father, Hecatomnus, was the king of Caria. Caria was part of the vast Persian Empire. The Persian Empire included the modern countries of Iran, Turkey, Egypt, Syria, and northern India. Although Caria was part of the empire, it operated as an independent kingdom.

Mausolus was Hecatomnus's oldest son. When Hecatomnus died in 377 B.C., Mausolus became king of Caria. Mausolus chose to make Halicarnassus the capital city of Caria. Halicarnassus's modern name is Bodrum, Turkey.

During his reign, Mausolus made the kingdom of Caria richer and larger. For example, his armies conquered towns and cities in the region and made them part of Caria. Halicarnassus had a harbor, and Mausolus made it an important port for trade ships.

To protect Halicarnassus, Mausolus built huge defensive walls around the city. The walls had watchtowers from which soldiers could scan the surrounding lands and sea. But Mausolus also wanted to make Halicarnassus a great city. He built a huge palace, where he lived with his wife, Queen Artemisia. He and Artemisia built public buildings, such as theaters and

FAMOUS *Mausoleums*

King Mausolus's tomb is not the world's only famous mausoleum. The Taj Mahal in Agra, India, is a mausoleum. It was built for Queen Mumtaz Mahal in the A.D. 1600s. In the United States, a well-known mausoleum is Grant's Tomb in New York City. Ulysses S. Grant was a general in the American Civil War (1861–1865) and was the eighteenth U.S. president (1869–1877). In Moscow, Russia, Lenin's Tomb *(below)* holds the body of V. I. Lenin, who ruled that country from 1917 until 1924.

Left: *This statue of Mausolus stood in his Mausoleum at Halicarnassus.* Right: *This sixteenth-century French illustration of Artemisia shows her holding an urn. The image was created for a book on the lives of famous women.*

FAST *Fact*

Hecatomnus and Mausolus were known as satraps. A satrap was a ruler of a small division of the Persian Empire. Most satraps were very powerful rulers in their region.

temples. They paved the streets of Halicarnassus and built houses for the people of the city.

During this time, Mausolus began building a tomb for himself. He wanted it to be very big and very beautiful—a fitting memory for a great king. He chose to build the tomb on a hill overlooking Halicarnassus. People could see the hilltop from a great distance. When the tomb was complete, people would be able to see it from far away.

A Beautiful Building

Mausolus died before his tomb was built. But Artemisia carried out his plans. She hired famous architects and artists from Greece to finish the building. It took more than three years to build. The tomb was complete by 350 B.C.

The tomb stood 140 feet (45 m) high, as high as a modern fourteen-story building. One side was 120 feet (40 m) long. The other side was 100 feet (33 m) long. Along each outer wall, rows of columns supported a pointed roof. A statue of Mausolus in a chariot pulled by four horses may have stood on the peak of the roof.

Artists also put up statues between the stone columns on each side of the building. Some statues were life-sized carvings of people. Others showed gods that people worshipped in that region in ancient times. There even were statues of lions, horses, and other animals.

Carvings on the building's sides told the story of battles. Statues and pictures carved from a flat surface are called bas-reliefs. The mausoleum's bas-reliefs were carved by four of the region's most famous artists—Leochares, Bryaxis, Scopas, and Timotheus. Hundreds of other artists and workers also helped decorate the tomb.

THE QUEEN'S *Surprise*

When the people of Rhodes heard that Mausolus was dead, they decided to attack Halicarnassus. Mausolus had conquered their island near Greece. Halicarnassus was without a king, so Rhodes decided to get even. They sent warships up the coast of Turkey toward Mausolus's city.

Queen Artemisia found out that the Rhodes fleet was on its way. She ordered her own warships to hide outside the city's harbor. When the Rhodes ships arrived at Halicarnassus, no one tried to stop them. Rhodian soldiers jumped off their ships to fight with Artemisia's soldiers inside the city.

Meanwhile, Artemisia's ships sailed back into the harbor. Her sailors boarded the empty Rhodian ships and sailed back to Rhodes. When the ships arrived, people in Rhodes thought it was their own victorious fleet. They celebrated and welcomed the ships into the harbor. But the people were shocked as Artemisia's soldiers jumped off the docked ships. The soldiers swarmed into Rhodes and conquered the island again.

Top: *This seventeenth-century French painting shows Artemisia speaking with the architects who are building her husband's tomb.* Left: *Archaeologists reconstructed this colossal horse from fragments found at the site of the Mausoleum at Halicarnassus.*

> *"Nothing is equal to [the mausoleum] either in size or in beauty. It is enriched with the most perfect works of art, with statues of men and horses of costly marble, such as can hardly be found in temples, so that it is the perfect model for all tombs."*
>
> —*Lucian of Samosata, Assyrian (ancient Middle Eastern) writer, ca. A.D. 170*

Queen Artemisia never saw the mausoleum's full beauty. She died one year before the tomb was completed. Artemisia was probably buried in the tomb with Mausolus.

A WONDER IN RUINS

The mausoleum stayed in good condition for almost 1,600 years. But in the A.D. 1200s, earthquakes badly damaged the building. Some of it was knocked in pieces to the ground.

In the early 1400s, crusaders invaded the area around Caria. Crusaders were soldiers from western European lands such as England and Germany. These European armies tried to recapture Christian holy places from Muslim Arab conquerors. The crusaders built a castle near Halicarnassus. In 1494 they decided to make the castle bigger. They used stones from the ruined mausoleum for their building project.

Over the years, the crusaders took the mausoleum apart. By 1522 most

SHE MUST HAVE *Loved Him*

After King Mausolus died, his body probably was cremated (burned into ashes). One legend says that Queen Artemisia mixed some of the ash with spices. Artemisia stirred the ash and spices into water. The legend says that Artemisia then drank the water *(below, in a sixteenth-century German engraving).*

This crusader castle was built in 1402 and enlarged in the fifteenth century. It was built using the stones from the ruins of the Mausoleum at Halicarnassus. The large number of sailboats reflects the popularity of the harbor as well as the modern city of Bodrum.

of the blocks were recycled into the fort. Some of the mausoleum's beautiful marble carvings became wall decorations.

DID YOU *Know?*

The ancient Greek writer Herodotus made one of the first lists of the Seven Wonders. Herodotus was born in Halicarnassus about 480 B.C. At that time, Artemisia was still building Mausolus's tomb.

DIGGING THE MAUSOLEUM

Decorations reused in the castle help us understand how the mausoleum looked. Other important information came from the work of later archaeologists. Several teams searched for remains of the mausoleum. British archaeologist Sir Charles Newton led one such team. In

Tourists can visit the ruins of the Mausoleum at Halicarnassus in Turkey. Most of what can be seen is fallen pillars.

1857 Newton found a huge stone statue on the former site of the mausoleum.

Nearby was a huge stone statue of a woman. Newton thought these were statues of Mausolus and Artemisia. Newton sent the statues to the British Museum in London, England. Those statues and other artifacts of the mausoleum are on display in the British Museum.

Visitors to Turkey can see other remains of the Mausoleum at Halicarnassus. The crusader's castle, known as Bodrum Castle, still stands. It is used as an archaeology museum and is open to tourists looking for a glimpse of one of the Seven Wonders of the Ancient World.

How Do They
Know That?

Some of the best information about the mausoleum's appearance comes from Danish archaeologists led by Christian Jeppesen. Jeppesen and his team studied the remains of the mausoleum from 1966 to 1977. They wrote seven books about what the mausoleum was like. Other Danish archaeologists continued excavations of the mausoleum ruins in the 1990s.

This German engraving of the Mausoleum at Halicarnassus is from a series on the Seven Wonders of the Ancient World. It was created in the late nineteenth century.

6

THE Statue of Zeus AT OLYMPIA

$\mathcal{T}$HE OLYMPICS ARE A FAMOUS MODERN SPORTS EVENT. THE BEST ATHLETES FROM AROUND THE WORLD GATHER IN ONE COUNTRY. THEY COMPETE IN EVENTS SUCH AS SWIMMING, DIVING, SKIING, AND RUNNING. ALMOST FOUR BILLION PEOPLE WATCHED THE 2006 OLYMPICS ON TELEVISION.

The beginnings of the Olympic Games are almost three thousand years old. The games began in about 775 B.C. in Olympia, a city on the western coast of Greece. Olympia became famous as a sports center and as a holy place. To honor a Greek god, the people of the city built one of the Seven Wonders of the Ancient World—the Statue of Zeus at Olympia.

THE KING OF THE GODS

In Greek myth, Zeus lived on Mount Olympus with his wife, Hera. The ancient Greeks had many gods and goddesses, and they were all important in Greek religion. But Zeus was the king of the gods.

The ancient Olympic Games were held in honor of Zeus. People came to Olympia to watch contests between the best athletes in the world. While there, they also honored Zeus and other deities (gods and goddesses) in the city's many shrines and temples (holy buildings).

At first, the shrines were small and very simple. As time passed, however, more and more people visited Olympia. The city began to grow, as townspeople built places for visitors to stay and eat.

The city's shrines and temples grew larger and more elaborate. Local rulers decided that Olympia especially needed a bigger and better shrine to Zeus, the patron of their games. The rulers wanted the shrine to have a statue. They wanted a big, incredible statue that suited the king of the gods.

This Greek vase from the sixth-century B.C. shows a discus thrower.

HOW DO THEY *Know That?*

We know how Phidias built the Statue of Zeus at Olympia because archaeologists found the remains of his workshop. In the 1950s, they dug down into the soil at Olympia. The archaeologists found tools and other instruments that Phidias used to build the statue. From those artifacts, they learned about the technology Phidias used to make this wonder of the ancient world.

AN AMAZING WORKSHOP

The city leaders picked a sculptor named Phidias to make the statue. Phidias lived in Greece's capital city, Athens. He had just finished working on the Parthenon—a famous shrine on a hill above Athens.

When Phidias arrived in Olympia, he hired workers. They built a workshop. Work on the statue started between 470 and 460 B.C.

Phidias had invented a new method for building statues. First, he built a wooden framework inside the temple where the statue would stand. The framework was like a skeleton. It formed the rough shape of the statue.

Workers then carved and shaped pieces from different materials. For Zeus's clothing, workers used sheets of gold. For the god's skin, Phidias chose ivory. Ivory is a creamy white material made from the tusks (large teeth) of certain animals. Phidias invented a way to make ivory look just like fine marble.

ASSEMBLING A GOD

After the sheets of gold and ivory were shaped, Phidias and his workers took the pieces to the temple. They attached the pieces to the statue's framework. Phidias attached them so that the joints (seams) between each piece did not show. The statue's surface gleamed like polished stone. Zeus looked as if he had been carved out of a solid block of marble.

The statue sat on a carved wooden base about 20 feet (6.5 m) wide and 3 feet (1 m) high. Above that, Zeus was seated on a large throne. He rose almost 40 feet (12 m) above the base. That is as tall as a four-story building.

In his left hand, Zeus held a small statue of Nike, the goddess of victory. Zeus held a king's scepter (staff) with an eagle on top.

To finish the statue, Phidias carved animals and flowers on Zeus's gold robe and sandals. He added jewels and precious stones that glittered in the torchlight of the temple.

Daring to Ask Zeus

Phidias designed Zeus's temple to show the god's power. Imagine how athletes and other worshippers must have felt. They seemed tiny in front of the huge, powerful god. They humbled themselves before the statue and asked Zeus to help them win the Olympics.

Zeus continued to awe athletes and worshippers for eight hundred years. But over time, new rulers and new religions took over in Greece.

Did You Know?

In Greek myth, Nike helped people win in wars and in sporting events. Nike also served Zeus and drove his chariot. The sculpture of Nike shown below (its head broken off) is called Victory of Samothrace. The statue is from the second century B.C. and is at the Louvre Museum in Paris, France.

This color engraving came from a nineteenth-century German collection on the Seven Wonders of the Ancient World.

> *"He [Phidias, who designed the statue] has shown Zeus seated, but with his head almost touching the ceiling, so that we have the impression that if Zeus moved to stand up he would unroof the temple."*
>
> —Greek writer Strabo, ca. A.D. 20

In A.D. 391, those rulers banned the Olympic Games. They closed all the temples to the old gods—including the Temple of Zeus at Olympia.

ZEUS MOVES OUT

The Greeks decided to move the statue of Zeus out of the temple. They moved the king of the gods to a new palace in the city of Constantinople. In modern times, that city was renamed Istanbul, Turkey.

The move to Constantinople saved Zeus's statue. After the move, natural disasters destroyed most of Olympia. Earthquakes, floods, and landslides buried the ancient sports center. Layers of mud and dirt covered the ruins of the Temple of Zeus.

But in the end, even the king of the gods could not escape destruction. In 462 a fire burned down Zeus's palace in Constantinople and destroyed the statue.

SCIENTISTS MOVE IN

In 1829 archaeologists from France started excavating at Olympia. They carefully removed the dirt that covered the town. Underneath the ground, they located parts of the Temple of Zeus. Scientists also found broken pieces of statues. The statues may have been inside the temple. Those artifacts from Olympia were put on display in the Louvre Museum in Paris, France.

A BURNING *Event*

One early Olympic event took place right outside the temple. To show respect for Zeus, people sacrificed (killed) one hundred oxen. They burned the oxen and left the ashes for Zeus. Over hundreds of years, a huge pile of ashes built up.

These giant columns are all that remains of the magnificent Temple of Zeus.

Over the years, many other teams of scientists uncovered more of Olympia and the temple. Their findings provided important information about the temple. Other information came from images of the temple. Some images had survived on ancient works of art. Others were on ancient coins. Together with ancient writings, the images provided many clues about the wondrous Statue of Zeus at Olympia.

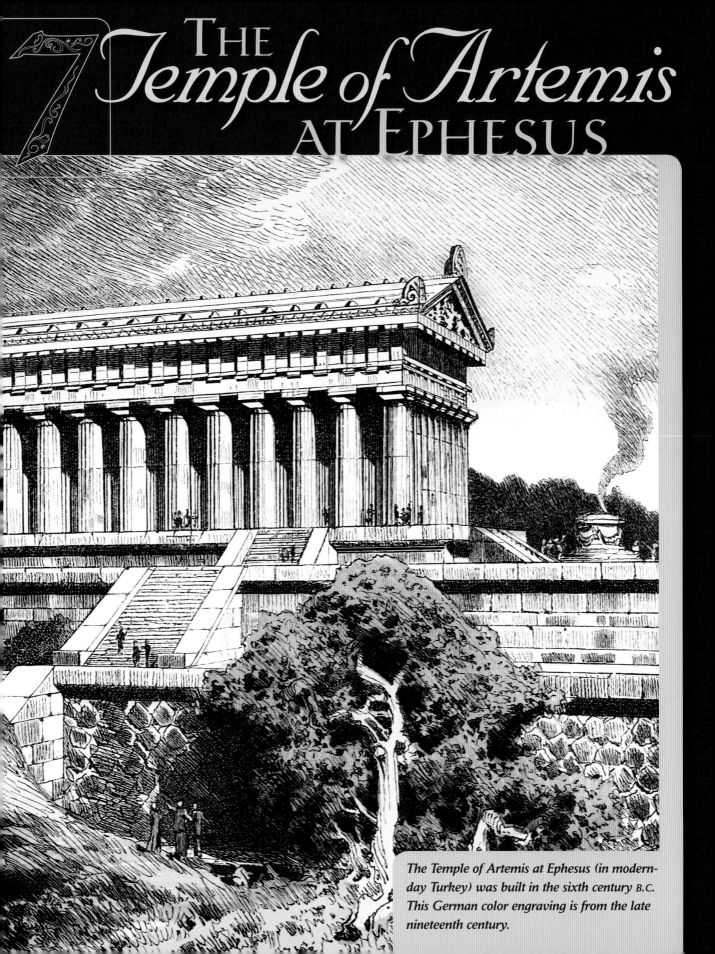

7 The Temple of Artemis at Ephesus

The Temple of Artemis at Ephesus (in modern-day Turkey) was built in the sixth century B.C. This German color engraving is from the late nineteenth century.

$\mathcal{P}$EOPLE IN THE ANCIENT WORLD WORSHIPPED MANY DIFFERENT GODS. CITIES BUILT TEMPLES IN HONOR OF THE GODS. ONE OF THESE TEMPLES WAS BUILT AT EPHESUS FOR ARTEMIS, AN ANCIENT GODDESS. IT BECAME ONE OF THE SEVEN WONDERS OF THE ANCIENT WORLD.

"*I have set eyes on the wall of lofty Babylon ... and the statue of Zeus ... and the hanging gardens, and the Colossus of the Sun [of Rhodes], and the huge ... high pyramids [at Giza], and the vast tomb of Mausolus. ...But when I saw the [Temple] of Artemis that mounted to the clouds ... those other marvels lost their brilliancy, and I said, '... the sun never looked on anything so grand.'*"

—*Antipater of Sidon, a Greek writer, ca. 100 B.C.*

Some of these places to worship the gods were quite small. They might have been just small mud or wooden buildings with a single statue of a god. Other temples were large and beautiful. They were built from fine marble and had many statues. People who visited temples all over the ancient Mediterranean world agreed on one thing. They said that Artemis's temple in the city of Ephesus was an amazing sight.

THE GODDESS

In ancient times, Turkey was part of a region known as Asia Minor. Beginning in the 900s B.C., Greek people crossed the Aegean Sea to settle along the west coast of Asia Minor. The Greeks settling in Ephesus found that the people there worshipped an ancient goddess. She was a mother goddess—the giver of life.

TWO Goddesses

In Greek art, Artemis is often shown as an athletic young woman. She carries a bow and arrow and often has a deer at her feet. The goddess of Ephesus looked nothing like this. Why does the Ephesian Artemis look so different from other Greek images of the goddess? Researchers believe that the Ephesian Artemis kept some of the features of older goddesses from Asia Minor. For example, the Ephesian Artemis is often linked with Cybele. Cybele was an ancient mother goddess from western Asia Minor. Her symbols included wild animals and bees.

Left: *This statue of Artemis came from Ephesus. The Ephesian Artemis was a symbol of fertility as well as hunting.* Right: *This is a copy of a fourth-century B.C. Greek sculpture of Artemis.*

Ancient statues showed the goddess with breasts or eggs covering her body. Those objects symbolized fertility.

The goddess reminded the Greeks of one of their own deities—Artemis. In ancient Greek mythology, Artemis was the goddess of wild animals and hunting. She was also the goddess of childbirth. The connection between motherhood and childbirth linked the two goddesses. And both goddesses were associated with animals. The Greeks began calling the Ephesian goddess Artemis.

A Rich Ruler

Over the centuries, Ephesus grew into a large city in Greek Asia Minor. It was located at what people then thought was the center of the world. Many of the main roads in the region passed through Ephesus. Travelers naturally stopped in Ephesus during their journeys. The city also was an important port. Ships from around the world sailed to and from its harbor.

People also came to Ephesus to worship Artemis. Temples to Artemis had stood in the same spot in Ephesus since about 800 B.C. The early temples were small and simple. People came there to say prayers to the goddess. They also offered the goddess gifts of flowers or food.

About 560 B.C., a powerful ruler named Croesus took control of Ephesus. Croesus was king of Lydia, an ancient country located in present-day northwestern Turkey. Croesus took over many of the cities along the west coast of Asia Minor. He was happy to conquer Ephesus, with its busy seaport.

Croesus was very wealthy. He was known throughout the region for his enormous stores of treasure and for his beautiful palace in the ancient city of Sardis. Croesus decided to spend some of his wealth in Ephesus. He decided to build a huge new temple for Artemis. He hired a famous Greek architect, Chersiphron, to design the temple.

A Wonderful Temple

Ancient writers gave different descriptions of the temple's size. The Roman writer Pliny said it was enormous—377 feet (115 m) long and 180 feet (55 m) wide.

The columns were one of the most wondrous parts of this temple. The temple had 127 marble columns. Each column was about 60 feet (18 m) high. The columns were arranged in rows along each of the temple's sides. They were slender, with a beautifully carved design.

Designs also were carved into the temple's marble pediments. A pediment is a triangular piece on the front of a building, where the two sides of a roof meet.

Inside the temple, artists carved statues of Artemis. One huge statue stood in the very center of the temple. On many temple statues of Artemis, the upper part of the goddess is covered in egg-shaped carvings (which some researchers think are breasts). From the stomach down, her body is enclosed in a straight pillar. Carvings of animals and bees cover the pillar. The crown on Artemis's head is shaped like the walls of the city.

This drawing of the Temple of Artemis at Ephesus comes from an American text called Wonders of the Past, *published in the early twentieth century.*

DESTRUCTION OF THE TEMPLE

The beautiful building brought even more people to Ephesus to worship Artemis. When visitors went home, they told stories about the amazing city and its temple. Soon, Ephesus became a popular tourist spot. People on the street sold food, drinks, and souvenirs to the tourists. Visitors may have bought drawings or small carved copies of the temple.

But the popular temple drew the wrong kind of attention in 356 B.C. That year a man named Herostratus crept up to the temple in the dark of a summer night. He climbed the stairs inside the temple and set fire to the roof's wooden frame. As the fire raged across the roof, the heat began cracking the marble columns. Ephesians watched in horror as the temple came tumbling down.

Herostratus did not try to escape after setting the fire. In fact, he was proud of what he had done. He told people that he had burned down the temple to become famous. He wanted his name known throughout the world as the destroyer of Artemis's great temple.

THE RUINS OF A WONDER

About 334 B.C., the rulers of Ephesus decided to rebuild the temple. Rebuilding took many years. The new temple was large and beautiful like the previous temple. But it was destroyed by an army that invaded Ephesus in

HOW DO THEY *Know That?*

British archaeologist John Turtle Wood helped us understand how the Temple of Artemis looked. In 1863 the British Museum in London sent Wood to Ephesus to find the temple's remains.

Wood had no idea where the temple was. His workers dug in one spot and then another for six years. Finally, in 1869, they found the remains of the great temple. They eventually dug a hole 300 feet (91 m) wide and 500 feet (152 m) long.

The workers found beautiful artifacts and sent them back to the British Museum. Those artifacts are still on display.

In 1904 other British Museum archaeologists returned to Ephesus. From their work, we know that five temples had been built at the site. The temples were built one on top of the other.

A.D. 262. People began taking broken stone and marble from the temple site. They used it to build forts and roads. After Christianity arrived in the area, pieces of the temple were used to build churches. Only one of the temple's original 127 columns remains. It still stands in a field of grass littered with ancient stone building blocks.

Modern tourists can visit the site of the Temple of Artemis at Ephesus. It sits close to the Turkish town of Selcuk. Signs at the site show how the temple probably looked when it was a great center for worship. The Ephesus Museum is also nearby. It holds many artifacts and treasures of the ancient city's history.

One standing column is all that remains of the Temple of Artemis at Ephesus.

TIMELINE

CA. 2920 B.C.	Pharaohs begin ruling ancient Egypt.
CA. 2551	The pharaoh Khufu begins building the Great Pyramid at Giza.
CA. 1700	Babylonians settle in Mesopotamia. An early Babylonian king, Hammurabi, creates a set of laws known as the Code of Hammurabi.
900s	Greek people settle in Asia Minor (modern-day Turkey), in cities such as Ephesus.
CA. 775	The Olympic Games begin in Olympia, Greece. They are held to honor the Greek god Zeus.
CA. 600	Nebuchadnezzar II begins building the Hanging Gardens of Babylon for his wife, Amyitis.
CA. 560	Croesus, a ruler in Asia Minor, takes control of Ephesus. He begins building a large temple to the Greek goddess Artemis in the city.
CA. 470	The Greek sculptor Phidias begins work on the Statue of Zeus at Olympia in Greece.
CA. 450	Greek historian Herodotus visits the Great Pyramid at Giza.
377	Mausolus became king of Caria, an ancient region of Turkey. He begins building an enormous tomb for himself, but he dies before it is complete.
356	An Ephesian named Herostratus destroys the Temple of Artemis at Ephesus.
350	Artemisia, Mausolus's wife, finishes the tomb. It becomes known as the Mausoleum at Halicarnassus.
CA. 334	The rulers of Ephesus begin building a new Temple of Artemis.
CA. 332	The reign of Egyptian pharaohs ends. Alexander the Great founds the city of Alexandria, Egypt.
306	Ptolemy I Soter makes himself king of Egypt. The people of Rhodes declare their support for Ptolemy.
305	One of Ptolemy's rivals, Demetrius, begins attacking Rhodes. After a year, he withdraws his army.
294	The people of Rhodes begin building the colossus to thank the sun god Helios for his help during the war against Demetrius.
CA. 290	Ptolemy I Soter begins building a giant lighthouse on the island of Pharos just outside Alexandria, Egypt. He dies before the Lighthouse at Alexandria is finished.
285	Ptolemy II officially opens the Lighthouse at Alexandria.
282	The Colossus of Rhodes is finished.

225	An earthquake strikes Rhodes and destroys the colossus.
A.D. 262	An invading army destroys the second Temple of Artemis at Ephesus.
391	Greek rulers ban the Olympic Games and close the Temple of Zeus at Olympia. Zeus's followers move his statue to Constantinople (present-day Istanbul, Turkey).
462	A fire destroys Zeus's statue in Constantinople.
654	Arab armies conquer Rhodes and sell pieces of the colossus as scrap metal.
1200s	Earthquakes badly damage the Mausoleum at Halicarnassus.
CA. 1303	The Lighthouse at Alexandria is destroyed by an earthquake.
1480	Sultan Quait Bey of Egypt builds a military fort in Alexandria using stones from the ruined lighthouse.
1494	European crusaders (soldiers) use pieces of the Mausoleum at Halicarnassus to build a castle in Bodrum, Turkey.
1829	French archaeologists start excavating at Olympia, Greece. They discover the ruins of the Temple of Zeus.
1857	British archaeologist Sir Charles Newton finds a huge stone statue on the site of the Mausoleum at Halicarnassus.
1869	British archaeologist John Turtle Wood finds the remains of an enormous temple at the site of the ancient city of Ephesus. Other British archaeologists later find the ruins of four other temples at the same spot.
CA. 1905	German archaeologist Robert Koldewey begins excavating (digging up) the remains of what he believes are the Hanging Gardens of Babylon.
1950s	Archaeologists excavating Olympia, Greece, find tools and other instruments that Phidias used to build the Statue of Zeus at Olympia.
1966	Danish archaeologists begin studying the remains of the Mausoleum at Halicarnassus.
1994	Underwater archaeologists discover huge stone blocks from the Lighthouse at Alexandria in the seas around Pharos.
2006	A group of panelists for *Good Morning America* (a U.S. television show) and *USA Today* (a U.S. newspaper) choose a list of New Seven Wonders of the World.
2007	NewOpenWorld Foundation, a Swiss organization, conducts a worldwide poll to choose the New Seven Wonders of the World.

CHOOSE AN EIGHTH WONDER

Now that you've read about the Seven Wonders of the Ancient World, do a little research to choose an eighth wonder. Or make a list with your friends, and vote to see which wonder is the favorite.

To do your research, look at some of the websites and books listed in the Further Reading and Websites sections of this book. Look for places in the ancient world that
• *have a cool history*
• *were difficult to make at the time or required new technology*
• *were extra big or tall*
• *were hidden from view or unknown to foreigners for many centuries*

You might even try gathering photos and writing your own chapter on the eighth wonder!

GLOSSARY AND PRONUNCIATION GUIDE

Alexandria (a-lig-ZAN-dree-uh): a city in the country of Egypt founded by Alexander the Great in 332 B.C.

archaeologist: a scientist who studies buildings, tools, and other remains of ancient civilizations

architect: a person who designs buildings and often oversees their construction

Artemis (AHR-tuh-muhs): the ancient Greek goddess of fertility, childbirth, and hunting

Babylon (BA-buh-lahn): an ancient city in Babylonia (part of the modern country of Iraq)

colossus: a gigantic statue or monument

Ephesus (EH-fuh-suhs): an ancient city located in present-day Turkey

excavate: to dig up artifacts that have been buried underground

Giza (GEE-zuh): an ancient town on the Nile River in northern Egypt

Halicarnassus (ha-luh-kahr-NA-suhs): an ancient city that stood on the site of present-day Bodrum, Turkey

Herodotus (hih-RAH-duh-tuhs): an ancient Greek writer known for his many travels and for his descriptions of the wonders of the ancient world

lighthouse: a high building topped by a bright light that shows safe routes for ships at sea

mastabas: low, rectangular buildings in ancient Egypt. Pharaohs and other important people were buried in mastabas.

mausoleum (maw-suh-LEE-uhm): a building that serves as a tomb

Olympia (uh-LIM-pee-uh): a town in Greece where the Olympic Games began about 775 B.C.

pharaohs: rulers in ancient Egypt from about 2920 to 332 B.C.

pyramid: a four-sided building that comes to a point at the top

tomb: a place, often a building, where dead people are buried

Zeus (ZOOS): the king of the ancient Greek gods

Source Notes

12 Herodotus, quoted in M. I. Finley, ed., *The Portable Greek Historians: The Essence of Herodotus, Thucydides, Xenophon, Polybius* (1959; repr., New York: Penguin Books, 1977), 54.

24 Pliny the Elder, *Natural History*, trans. John F. Healy (London: Penguin Books, 1991), 313.

28 Plutarch, *The Life of Alexander the Great,* ed. Arthur Hugh Clough, trans. John Dryden (New York, Modern Library, 2004), 26–27.

30 Jimmy Dunn, "Pharos Lighthouse of Alexandria," *Tour Egypt*, n.d., http://www.touregypt.net/featurestories/pharoslighthouse.htm (February 12, 2008).

37 Herodotus, quoted in Carol Strickland, *The Annotated Arch: A Crash Course in the History of Architecture* (Kansas City, MO: Andrews McNeel, 2001), 6.

40 Strabo, quoted in Robert Lee Morrell, *Genesis Unveiled* (Victoria, BC: Trafford Publishing, 2005), 151.

50 W. R. Lethaby, *The Tomb of Mausolus* (London: B.T. Batsford, 1908), available online at http://penelope.uchicago.edu/Thayer/E/Gazetteer/Places/Europe/Turkey/_Periods/Greek/_Texts/LETGKB/Mausoleum*.html (February 12, 2008).

60 Strabo, quoted in Angus Konstam, *Historical Atlas of Ancient Greece* (London: Mercury Books, 2005), 182.

64 Antipater, quoted in Ben Witherington III, ed., *History, Literature, and Society of the Book of Acts* (Cambridge: Cambridge University Press, 1996), 273.

SELECTED BIBLIOGRAPHY

Bahn, Paul G., ed. *The Cambridge Illustrated History of Archaeology.* Cambridge: Cambridge University Press, 1999.

Burton, Rosemary, and Richard Cavendish. *Wonders of the World: 100 Great Man-Made Treasures of Civilization.* New York: Metro Books, 2003.

Cantor, Norman F. *Antiquity: The Civilization of the Ancient World.* New York: HarperCollins, 2003.

Clayton, Peter, and Martin Price, eds. *The Seven Wonders of the Ancient World.* New York: Routledge, 1989.

Harris, Stephen L. "Seven Wonders of the Ancient World." In *The Wonders of the World.* Washington, DC: National Geographic Society, 1998.

Jordan, Paul. *The Seven Wonders of the Ancient World.* Harlow, UK: Longman, 2002.

Reader's Digest Editors. *Vanished Civilizations.* New York: Reader's Digest, 2002.

Romer, John, and Elizabeth Romer. *The Seven Wonders of the World: A History of Modern Imagination.* London: Seven Dials, 2000.

Scarre, Chris, ed. *The Seventy Wonders of the Ancient World: The Great Monuments and How They Were Built.* London: Thames & Hudson, 2000.

Stefoff, Rebecca. *Finding the Lost Cities.* New York: Oxford University Press, 1997.

FURTHER READING AND WEBSITES

Books

Ash, Russell. *Great Wonders of the World.* New York: Dorling Kindersley, 2000. Ash provides a strong foundation for students learning about both ancient and modern constructions. The illustrations give readers a glimpse into the beautiful buildings of the world.

Calliope Magazine. Peterborough, NH: Cobblestone Publishing. *Calliope Magazine* provides a wide variety of articles about ancient civilizations for readers ages nine to fourteen.

Day, Nancy. *Your Travel Guide to Ancient Egypt.* Minneapolis: Twenty-First Century Books, 2001. Pack your bags for a trip back to ancient Egypt. Learn about Egyptian history, customs, food, famous sites, and much more.

———. *Your Travel Guide to Ancient Greece.* Minneapolis: Twenty-First Century Books, 2001. Get your passport to history ready for a trip back to ancient Greece. Learn about local customs, food, famous sites, and much more.

McIntosh, Jane. *Eyewitness Books: Archaeology.* New York: Alfred A. Knopf, 1994. McIntosh provides a broad overview of the field of archaeology with easily understood explanations about how scientists learn about other civilizations. Photographs of many artifacts and sites provide an exciting picture of earlier civilizations.

National Geographic Investigates series. Washington, DC: National Geographic Children's Books, 2006. This series of books looks at how archaeology can unlock the secrets of ancient civilizations, such as ancient Greece and ancient Egypt.

Visual Geography series. Minneapolis: Twenty-First Century Books, 2003–2009. Each book in this series details the geography, history, culture, and economy of a different country, including Egypt, Iraq, and Turkey.

Woods, Michael, and Mary B. Woods. *Ancient Construction: From Tents to Towers.* Minneapolis: Twenty-First Century Books, 2000. Find out about the construction techniques used in the ancient world.

Websites

The British Museum: Ancient Greece

http://www.ancientgreece.co.uk/

This British Museum site is one of the best online sources for ancient Greece. It provides a broad overview of ancient Greek culture. Sections include a list and explanation of gods and goddesses and a geography section with maps of famous sites and Greek colonies.

Seven Wonders of the Ancient World Tour

http://www.unmuseum.org/wonders.htm

The UnMuseum offers a virtual tour—with plenty of detailed information—of each of the Seven Wonders of the Ancient World.

Seven Wonders of the World

http://www.hillmanwonders.com/z_seven_wonders/seven_wonders.htm

This website is run by travel authority Howard Hillman. It includes interesting tidbits and fun quizzes about the seven wonders. It also includes numerous links to other wonders and regions around the world.

Treasures of the Sunken City

http://www.pbs.org/wgbh/nova/sunken/wonders/

This companion site to an episode of the television program *Nova* includes illustrations of the Seven Wonders of the Ancient World. It also links to a modern scientific expedition to explore the waters of the harbor at Alexandria, Egypt. Scientists belief the underwater treasures, spread over more than 5 acres (2 hectares), include large architectural pieces of the Lighthouse at Alexandria.

Visual Geography Series

http://www.vgsbooks.com/

This extension of Lerner Publishing Group's Visual Geography Series® (VGS) is a one stop resource for links to additional country-specific information, up-to-date statistics, photographs and maps that can be downloaded, and much more.

INDEX

About the Authors

Michael Woods is a science and medical journalist in Washington, D.C., who has won many national writing awards. Mary B. Woods is a school librarian. Their previous books include the eight-volume Ancient Technology series, the Disasters Up Close series, *The History of Communication, The History of Medicine,* and *The Tomb of King Tutankhamen.* The Woodses have four children. When not writing, reading, or enjoying their grandchildren, the Woodses travel to gather material for future books.

Photo Acknowledgments

The images in this book are used with the permission of: © iStockphoto.com/Luke Daniek, p. 6; illustrations © Laura Westlund/ Independent Picture Service, pp. 7, 19, 27, 35, 45, 55, 63; © Kurt Scholz/SuperStock, p. 8; © Kenneth Garrett/Danita Delimont/Alamy, p. 9; © Kean Collection/ Hulton Archive/Getty Images, p. 10; © iStockphoto.com/Mehmet Faith Kocyildir, p. 13; © Bridgeman Art Library/Getty Images, p. 14 (top), 65 (right); © G.R. Richardson/SuperStock, p. 14 (bottom); ©Sylvain Grandadam/Photographer's Choice/Getty Images, p. 15 (top); © Panoramic Images/Getty Images, p. 15 (bottom); © Sylvain Grandadam/The Image Bank/Getty Images, p. 17; © Ferdinand Knab/The Bridgeman Art Library/Getty Images, pp. 18, 26, 53, 59, 62, 72 (center right); © Erich Lessing/Art Resource, NY, pp. 20, 56; © akg-images/Peter Connolly, p. 21; © Photodisc/Getty Images, p. 22; © Salvador Dali, Colossus of Rhodes, 1954, 68.8 x 39 cm, Oil on Canvas, Museum of Fine Arts Bern, Switzerland, p. 23; © istockphoto.com/ Ivo Velinov, p. 25; © istockphoto.com/Yiannis Papadimitriou, p. 28; © DEA/De Agostini Picure Library/ Getty Images, p. 29; The Art Archive/Archaeological Museum of Alexandria, p. 31 (top); The Art Archive/British Museum, p. 31 (bottom); © iStockphoto.com/zbruch, p. 32; © Mary Evans Picture Library/Alamy, pp. 34, 67, 72 (bottom right, bottom center, bottom left); © AFP /Getty Images, p. 36; The Art Archive/San Zeno Maggiore Verona Italy/Alfredo Dagli Orti, p. 37; ©DEA/ G. Dagli Orti/Drr, p. 38; ©DEA/C. SAPPA/Drr, p. 39; The Art Archive/British Library, p. 40; © DEA Picture Library/Drr, p. 41; The Art Archive/Abbey of Novacella or Neustift/Giani Dagli Orti, p. 43 (bottom); © Wilhelm van Ehrenberg/The Bridgeman Art Library/Getty Images, p. 44; © Douglas Armand/Stone/Getty Images, p. 46; © Scala/Art Resource, NY, p. 47 (left); The Art Archive/Musée Thomas Dobrée Nantes, p. 47 (right); akg-images/National Museum, p. 49 (top); © age fotostock/Superstock, p. 49 (bottom); The British Musuem, p. 50; © Ozerk Kalender/Alamy, p. 51; © Yoray Liberman/Getty Images, p. 52; © SuperStock, Inc./SuperStock, p. 54; © iStockphoto.com/Joan Coll, p. 57; © Reunion des Musees Nationaux/Art Resource, NY, p. 58; The Art Archive/Gianni Dagli Orti, pp. 43, 61; © Peter Horree/Alamy, p. 65 (left); © Roger Cracknell/Alamy, p. 69; © The Print Collector/Alamy, p. 72 (top right); © DEA/De Agostini Picure Library/Getty Images, p. 72 (top left), iStockphoto.com/Karim Hesham, p. 72 (top center).

Front Cover: © Ferdinand Knab/The Bridgeman Art Library/Getty Images (top left); © iStockphoto. com/Karim Hesham (top center); © The Print Collector/Alamy (top right); © Mary Evans Picture Library/Alamy (center, bottom left); © DEA Picture Library/De Agostini Picture Library/Getty Images (bottom center); © North Wind Pictures Archives/Alamy (bottom right).